FOREWORD

Here at Young Writers, we love to let imaginations run wild and creativity go crazy. Our aim is to encourage young people to get their creative juices flowing and put pen to paper. Each competition is tailored to the relevant age group, hopefully giving each pupil the inspiration and incentive to create their own piece of creative writing, whether it's a poem or a short story. By allowing them to see their own work in print, we know their confidence and love for the written word will grow.

For our latest competition Poetry Wonderland, we invited primary school pupils to create wild and wonderful poems on any topic they liked – the only limits were the limits of their imagination! Using poetry as their magic wand, these young poets have conjured up worlds, creatures and situations that will amaze and astound or scare and startle! Using a variety of poetic forms of their own choosing, they have allowed us to get a glimpse into their vivid imaginations. We hope you enjoy wandering through the wonders of this book as much as we have.

Oxfordshire

Edited By Debbie Killingworth

First published in Great Britain in 2019 by:

YoungWriters®
Est. 1991

Young Writers
Remus House
Coltsfoot Drive
Peterborough
PE2 9BF
Telephone: 01733 890066
Website: www.youngwriters.co.uk

CONTENTS

Lola Brown (10)	76
Justin Constantine Grimes (11)	77
Rose Macbeth-Benson (9)	78
Ben Barrie (9)	79
Kirsty Cleare (11)	80
Dylan Georgiou-White (10)	81
Joshua Lewis (9)	82
Caelyn Ferreira (9)	83
Katie Mace (9)	84
Calvin Schuman (9)	85
Finlay Ryan (10)	86
Róisín Caldwell (10)	87
Elodie Varnam (9)	88
Kris Toft (9)	89
Kai Green (9)	90
Grace Clark (10)	91

Chandlings School, Kennington

Georgia Wright (8)	92
Sophia Stewart (8)	94
Anastasiya Sinitsina (7)	96
Emmeline Pink (8)	97
Sofia Trajtenberg (8)	98
Louis Isaacs (8)	99
Arnav Jain (8)	100
Martha Payne (7)	101
Olivia Arbuckle (8)	102
Thomas Liddiard (8)	103
Charlotte Carter (8)	104
Andy Chengchao Xu (9)	105
Kiyan Irani (7)	106
Arianna Malmberg (8)	107
Helena Fleming (8)	108
Chloé Paulus (8)	109
Freya Osborne (8)	110
James Lee (7)	111
Jasper James Bromage (8)	112
Xanthe Hodgin (8)	113
Max Cavaliere (9)	114
Rufus Worrall (7)	115
Evie Jefferis (7)	116
Max Lucking (7)	117
Archie Warrilow (8)	118

Jaya R S Hill (7)	119
Ellie May Bromley (7)	120
Alice Carol Rendell (7)	121
Anur Nayak (8)	122
Pratiba Stewart (8)	123
Stella De Silva (7)	124
Holly Andrews (7)	125
Freddie Anders (7)	126
Felix Grund (8)	127
Sid Davies (8)	128
Laurence Maggs (7)	129
Claire Voillemont-Choi (9)	130
Ajeet Nagi (8)	131
Lara Galvani-Silva (8)	132
Josh (7)	133
Owais Faruq (9)	134
Zara Hartwright (8)	135
Jonny Hook (7)	136
Ellie Thorburn (8)	137
Belle White (7)	138
Isabella Ferrarese (7)	139

Great Milton CE Primary School, Oxford

Hollie Colverson (10)	140
Eva Lily Thatcher (10)	141
Charlie Morgan Lewis Groves (10)	142
Esmée Webb (10)	143
Scarlett Shorter (10)	144
Millie McCann (10)	145
Elda Parton (10)	146
Elliott Donald Flint Richardson (10)	147
Tiger-Lee Coombes (10)	148
Eden Adiri (10)	149
Harry Taylor (11)	150
Samuel Bridge (10)	151

Grove CE Primary School, Grove

| Elisha Fernandez (10) | 152 |
| Phoebe Miles (8) | 153 |

Lily Sutton (7)	154
Thomas L Reeves (10)	155
Megan Zamora Rowe (8)	156
Francesca Grace Huggins (7)	157
Aliceson Livingston (7)	158
Maizie Liverbeth (7)	159
Ava Sherriff (7)	160
Summer Carter (7)	161
Samuel (7)	162
Kayden Rowbottom (7)	163
Thomas Perkins (7)	164
Hannah Sear (7)	165
Joshua Norris (7)	166
Rudi Jenkins (8)	167

Wood Farm Primary School, Headington

Samrah Shah (10)	168
Alyssa Boyce Hall (9)	169
Dominik Ivancik (10)	170
Sienna Rowe (9)	171
Mya Evans (10)	172
Mohamed (9)	173
Harry Stillman (9)	174
Mitul Gupta (9)	175
Iman Zia (9)	176
Adina Nadeem-Aftab (9)	177
Haniya Khanum Siddique (10)	178
Camron Betnay (10)	179
Huda Boucetta (10)	180
Tawhida Al-Jannath (9)	181
Mohammed Siddiq (10)	182
Shania Darcy Lewis (10)	183
Rasjhad Kanbus (10)	184

The Poems

The Flight Of The Phoenix

One late afternoon,
I could almost see the moon,
Then there was a bright, colourful flash,
Followed by another bright, colourful flash.
I decided to run out the door,
And I couldn't believe what I saw...

A phoenix with one red feather,
The rest were orange due to the warm weather.
I wished to go and have a ride,
As flying myself I'd already tried.
Slowly I sat on for a turn,
Because wanting to fly, I decided to learn.

In the clouds we started to soar,
I could see everything on the floor,
Going up and up, we were high in the sky,
I could hear all the birds tweeting as we went by.

Giselle Molloholli (11)

Seasons

Spring is the season when everything starts to form again.
The trees are no longer bare as the baby leaves begin to grow.
The first flowers begin to sprout and finally, the sun comes out.

The next season is summer...
Summer is when we all go loose.
The children run around barefoot whilst the mums chit-chat in the sun,
dreading the end of the day when the ice cream truck comes to play.
The children daydream about the cold sweet taste, "Yum, yum," they say.

Autumn is the season when smiles on the children's faces begin to fade.
It's colder and the sun has gone but they still have time to play.
Let's go in the leaves, they say.

Winter is last on our list.

Winter is cold and icy but winter is fun.

The children get out their coats and go and make angels and statues in the frosted snow.

Dads groan about the deep cold feeling they have just been shown.

All the seasons play a role and they will all stay in your soul.

Isabella Verity Slater (10)

Aston & Cote CE Primary School, Aston

Angry Birds

Bang! The space pigs are invading
From their planet called The Pigs.
Their home was big, green and mouldy,
I wouldn't want that for my digs!

The pigs are coming,
Their spaceship whooshed,
Full speed ahead!
The Birds' planet was so colourful,
Blue and green, yellow and red!

The Space Pigs had one mission.
To steal the Birds' colourful eggs.
They were super good for eating
And gave them muscles in their legs!

But the Angry Birds were waiting,
They knew invasion was near.
They used a powerful slingshot,
To catch them in mid-air!

Euan Ross McDowell (7)
Aston & Cote CE Primary School, Aston

Emotion Poem

Loneliness is as grey as a storm.
It smells like a rotten egg.
It tastes like burnt toast.
It is pitch-black darkness.
It feels like a Chinese burn.
It sounds like an opera singer under attack.

Hope is as purple as a bat.
It tastes as sweet as toffee.
It smells like freshly baked bread.
It is a waterfall.
It feels like a fluffy cat.
It is the key to success.

Happiness is as yellow as a lemon.
It is as succulent as candyfloss.
It smells like sticky toffee pudding.
It is a rainbow.
It sounds like the first laugh of a baby.

Evie Walker (9)
Aston & Cote CE Primary School, Aston

The Whole World Above Me

There's a whole world above us,
Some that we can see,
But most of it is hidden
From children like you and me.

When I am older I would like to be an astronaut
So I can go and see
The shooting stars that look like racing cars,
The sparkling moon that looks like a big balloon.

There are aliens and rockets in astronauts' pockets
And amongst the stars, there are planets like Mars.

But most of all I would like to see
If there is another Isla, just like me.

Isla Poulsom (7)
Aston & Cote CE Primary School, Aston

The Sea

The sea, the sea, the beautiful blue sea,
You sparkle and glimmer when it's light
But you give a horrible fright at night.
When it's stormy you like to give the sailor a good
old fright,
But what happens when it is light?
When it is light you let all of the humans play
And have fun in you.
You are very extraordinary
Because you are one of God's most beautiful gifts.
The sea, the sea, the beautiful blue sea,
You really are a wonder to me.

Victoria Bungay (10)
Aston & Cote CE Primary School, Aston

What Is A Witch?

A witch's warts are as squishy as a pillow.
A witch's skin is as wrinkly as a shrivelled leaf.
A witch's voice is as croaky as a frog.
A witch's nose is as long as a stick.
A witch's hair is as scruffy as a scarecrow.
A witch's face is as green as grass.
A witch's hat is as pointy as a knife.
A witch's cloak billows in the breeze.
A witch's eyes are piercing and bright.
A witch's cat is as soft as a scarf.

Joseph George Slater (7)
Aston & Cote CE Primary School, Aston

Joplin

When Joplin runs at a fast pace
You can see her cute face.
She spies through the fur over her eyes
No one can see her looking at the pie.
Across the fields she likes to be wild
But only when it is quite mild.
Chasing geese and ducks off she goes
But when she stops no one knows.
Oh pretty Joplin with your pink bow
We always seem to be shouting, "Joplin, no!"
But Joplin with your messy fur
I really love you.

Bethany Sparrowhawk (10)
Aston & Cote CE Primary School, Aston

The Magic Sweety Land

Imagine if a whole world is made out of sweets.
Mouth-watering trees smell like candyfloss.
Stripy lollipops are stood like bushes.
The grass is made of delicious liquorice; green and thin.
The rainbow turned from hot, fiery red to watery blue.
Statues are made out of gummy bears
And every time you eat it, it grows back.
I could hear people laughing
Because they've had too many sweets.
This is a great world!

Samir Ali (7)

Aston & Cote CE Primary School, Aston

Swimming In A Sea Of Chocolate

Drip, drip, drip... the taste of chocolate on my lips.
Yum, yum, yum, the chocolate goes into my mouth and into my tum.
The sea of chocolate is smooth and brown.
The more I eat the more it weighs me down.
Swimming in a sea of chocolate is so fun and so nice.
I could do it every day, I could do it twice.
One day on Mars you will see me swimming in a sea of chocolate, happy as can be.

Charlotte Hickman (8)
Aston & Cote CE Primary School, Aston

The World Of Beauty

Smell the blossom
Climb the trees
Look at all the butterflies
And the bees.

Step outside
What can you see?
A world of beauty
Come with me.

Find a flower
Lovely and soft
How many of them can you spot?

Lie down, look at the clouds
What can you hear?
It is loud.

Beth Walker (7)
Aston & Cote CE Primary School, Aston

Dragons

D ragons are big and very scary
R acing green and ever so hairy
A stonishing, scaly and ever so quick
G igantic tongue ready to give you a lick
O bliterate everything in sight
N early always giving you a fright
S o that's why I love dragons.

Amelia Foster (8)
Aston & Cote CE Primary School, Aston

Demigod Adventures

An amazing feeling is what it is,
To be the son of the great god, Zeus.
Bending air and calling lightning
Are the mythical powers of the children of Zeus.
Monsters are attracted to my blood,
So it's likely you'll end up in a fight.
You may be able to take flight,
But they'll just track you down again.
Honestly, it's best to kill them at the start,
And then you will have played your part.

Hydras, Minotaurs that sort of stuff,
Will try to kill you,
The ugliest way possible.
Hydras spit acid and Minotaurs charge
But the one place you really don't want to go
Is the Underworld, I know!

That's where Hades lives with all his might.
He really loves to pick a fight.
Though there is one place worse,
Tarturus, the spirit of the abyss,

The husband of Gaia
And father of giants.

No living mortal ever goes down there,
Even the gods are too terrified,
The only things that are ever down there
Are monsters like Chimera,
And the king of the Titans, Kronos.

Gaia is evil, so evil
That she created and bred a race of giants
Which each had a purpose
To destroy a certain god,
Like Ephialtes and Otis were to destroy Dionysus,
Polybius to destroy Poseidon.

Alcyoneus to destroy Hades,
Porphyrion the king of the giants to destroy Zeus,
And Encialadys to destroy Athena.

Charles Bingham (9)
Barley Hill Primary School, Thame

Dragon Colourfully Stuck In A Rainbow

Happy as Larry, soaring,
In the sky as the rain was pouring,
The dragon found it a bit boring,
So he perched on the tree,
The dragon was up there
Feeling like he was going to fall off and about to wee.

Falling into a rainbow,
Terrified he knew,
He touched the rainbow,
His eye popped, showing them to the world.

He was lonely at first,
All curled up in a ball,
A scaly gold ball he was very bold,
All of a sudden he felt lonely and nervous.

The dragon's eye smashed out of the sockets
All the magical colours went into him,

He was sad and lonely,
However he figured out he was a rainbow,
He was so happy.

When he used all his force to escape,
He did not escape,
Randomly he was happy
That he was stuck,
I think it's because he can see the whole world.

He wandered up and down the rainbow,
Into the pot of gold
And he went to the other side of the rainbow.

All of a sudden he was hungry,
He wished for food and he got food,
He ate it in two seconds,
Randomly he really reminded me of a pig.

Happily, he figured out the sides of the rainbow
were slides,
Also, he thought the pot of gold was a big pillow,
To land on of course.

Chloe Hayes (10)
Barley Hill Primary School, Thame

Best Book Ever

Entering the colossal library,
Oliver walked down the aisle sadly,
Suddenly he found a mysterious book,
He took it off the shelf to have a look.

The book was by Stanley,
And to him there were symbols he could see,
He opened up to see an image,
The picture was of someone in red armour which
was damaged.

He suddenly turned into dust,
Which was the colour of rust,
Oliver met the man in the armour of red,
Looking at him he was almost half dead.

Crash! Bang! Walls fell,
Bltzzz! Oliver shot lightning and said, "What the
hell?"
Page after page was a new hero,
From Spider-Man to Black Panther.

At last he met his match,
Thor the thunderer who had a good catch,
He owns an axe named Stormbreaker,
Which was built by a dwarf maker.

Finally he had to exit the book,
He was happy and turned round to have a look,
Thousands of people were surprised,
Looking like they couldn't believe their eyes.

There was a smell which was disgusting,
And it wasn't anything from over there,
He looked down to find something new,
To find his trousers in wee and poo.

Thomas John Payne (11)
Barley Hill Primary School, Thame

The Adventures Of Coco Pops

T he elf is me in Coco Pops
H ey! I am surrounded by threats
E veryone is me in this box

A nd I will not get eaten
D o I start bouncing out the box
V itamin A is in Coco Pops, yay!
E xcuse me, this is my Coco Pop Land
N ow I am going out of the box
T ime to jump in, 3, 2, 1, *boom!*
U nder milk is more milk, oh no!
R acing and jumping into the milk.
E veryone thinks I am crazy, running and
      swimming in the milk
S omehow I am the milk, I love it!

O h yeah, this is fun!
F un I say, wow! I see a pancake.

C oco Pops, I am in a lake

O uch! Another Coco Pop got me!

C rack! I had a moment, use the bouncy pancake

O h, okay, I have left my friends in the sea

P op, crack! I am out

O h, bye Mummy, Shanae.

P opcorn is what I am going to be next year.

S ee you next time when I will hopefully be with the lot.

Ella Dymott (10)

Barley Hill Primary School, Thame

Roller Coaster Car

I woke up this morning,
To the fresh breeze of air,
I could smell my chocolate pancakes,
That are made downstairs.

I left for work,
Got in my car,
Put my keys in and...

The car shook,
The ground shook,
Metal poles rose,
A building surrounded me then closed,
I was trapped.

A door opened,
I moved,
Before me was a huge roller coaster,
Before I knew I was riding a roller coaster,
I thought it was great until I couldn't stop.

And I was looking at my watch,
I felt sick,

I could taste it in my mouth,
It was a roller coaster of emotions, literally.

I couldn't stop,
I panicked,
What did I do?
Pulled out the car keys.

Suddenly I fell back to the ground,
But then I woke up,
It was just a dream.

I had my toast,
Went to my car,
Put the keys in
And...

Mollie Price-Jones (10)
Barley Hill Primary School, Thame

The Future Tech Of Lava And Monsters

I woke feeling cheery and cold,
Ready for another day of green lava fun,
I zoomed down the zip wire
And the cold air stroked my face,
I landed in the mild warm, green lava,
Sloshing and boshing in the lava
I stopped for a drink,
But then I saw something wink.
I had dropped my drink.
Chasing after the thing that winked.
It flew into the colossal clouds,
I followed in my jetpack,
Pizza wafted the air,
My only way to chomp and chew on the pizza cloud,
The thing that winked flew around,
It was a magnificent beast,
Kind and friendly, a circular green monster with two teeth,
Fire eyes and green furry wings,

It stretched out a string-like arm,
And his chubby hand said, "Hi, I'm Bondz."
From that day on me and Bondz
Played in the green lava
And had mountains of fun.

Jack Turner (11)
Barley Hill Primary School, Thame

The Toadstool

There was a little toadstool
In the middle of an enchanted land,
The little fairies play in the sand,
There are lights and fun,
So you can play in the sun,
There are candyfloss trees
And there are fluffy bees.
In the toadstool there's fun, games and sweets,
Outside the toadstool are all different treats,
There's music in the toadstool,
You can dance and run,
In the toadstool there's room for everyone,
When you get to play,
You will want to stay,
You can buy genies as a pet,
Then you can stay till sunset,
All our food,
Get's you in your mood,
There are beds for you to sleep,
And windows you can peek,

When it gets late,
You say bye to your mate,
Goodbye.

Taylor Finch (9)
Barley Hill Primary School, Thame

Mythical Creatures In Candy Land

As the monsters go *crunch, crunch,*
The candy gets devoured.
The waterfall goes *drip, drip, drip,*
Everything is good.
The dragons go *flap, flap, flap.*
Eating the cotton candy clouds in the air.
Chocolate rockets collecting chocolate chips for
Cookie Land.
Mushrooms get eaten as they are only mushroom
candy.
Fluffy monsters looking for a new cave
They get loaded with edible things from different
planets, oh yummy,
Treasures get shared, everything is in harmony
Dragons give rides to creatures, cotton candy
clouds for everybody
Lollipop trees get sucked and sucked as chocolate
houses get built
Cookies and smores get eaten

Chocolate for everybody to share
Harmony is everywhere.

Zoe Rebecca Bayer (9)
Barley Hill Primary School, Thame

The Invasion Of The Food Minions

I entered KFC,
To see a burger in a seat,
All alone, no child to see.
I picked him up thinking he was a teddy
But to hear a child scream,
I became unsteady.
I looked down to see it was the burger teddy,
With what looked like a mini French fries teddy.

I couldn't tell as he shook his body,
Not letting go of his buddy.
I ran to my car to calm him down.

Once he was calm he told me his name,
Suddenly the pack of fries shouted,
"We are here to invade the planet,
And there's nothing you can do about it!"
Then they said, "There's two more,
A single French fry and a chicken nugget."

They then escaped out the window,
I never saw them again!

Olivia Clark (10)
Barley Hill Primary School, Thame

Frolicking On Mars

I skipped and frolicked about on Mars,
I couldn't even shout, "There's no cars!"
Sandy clouds surrounded me,
So aliens couldn't say, "There is she!"

Hovercraft hopped and leapt about,
Too fast for me to even shout,
"Hey, what are you doing up there?"
Perhaps we could even attempt a share?

I skipped and frolicked on a hydrogen cloud,
Not even complaining that it was very loud,
Sounds were horrid,
The bustling of aliens,
I wish I could be back on Earth,
Where I could be on good home Burf.

I should have checked the flights to Mars,
I should have known I couldn't buy cars,
For when I went I didn't know
How to get back to sew!

Natalie Oates (10)
Barley Hill Primary School, Thame

Hobs, Noggalys, Diddles Land

The blue fluffy Diddles were on their way home.
As the sky started pouring with Oreo snow.
The Noggalys were covered in candyfloss rain,
They were having a very bad day.
While the Diddles were warm at home,
The Noggalys were outside in the Oreo snow.
The Noggalys were not happy with what they were given,
The Hobs would never be forgiven.
The Diddles and Noggalys went to the Hobs,
They bought their bubble guns and their fun,
To show that they were not treated the same,
But from that day on nobody had to be in the snow again.

Everyone is the same Noggaly, Diddle, unicorn or human
We all deserve to be treated the same.

Nadja Williams (10)
Barley Hill Primary School, Thame

My Wings

With my wings,
I bounce across the clouds of China,
I touch the burning sun,
I watch the bustling crowds,
I sit with the pandas.

With my wings,
I skim the seas of Hawaii,
I surf the colossal waves,
I dive with the dolphins,
I dance on the sand.

With my wings,
I weave through the forests of Canada,
I perch on top of trees,
I ski down a sliding avalanche,
I run with a moose.

With my wings,
I frown at the rains of England,
I sit on top of London's time,
I hide in grey clouds,
I fly over the Thames.

With my wings,
I open my window,
I get back into bed,
I tell my mum, "Goodnight!"
I'm finally home!

Lucy Morris (10)
Barley Hill Primary School, Thame

Vegetable Vs Candy

A little squabble and a little food
Is all it takes to be rude
Worse and worse
The fight gets
Until both sides lets
For then declared the worst of war
Sealed by a roar.

Battles, betrayals and beating up
Much worse than an angry pup
Finally, one side gets the edge
In the battle near the hedge
Nearly there
Yay, they have won!

And on that day
It finally ends
The worst of war
The best of friends
All that gone
But one remains.
The candy reigns over the land

And now this poem
Is all done
From the veg
You must run
'Cause a second war
Will always come
Sweets Vs veg and candy won!

James Barnett (9)
Barley Hill Primary School, Thame

Chaotic Christmas Crisis

One Christmas morning,
I did a Christmas drawing
Then I got pulled into the world,
The only one with grass that's curled.

There was a sneaky spy,
Who seemed to be very shy,
Pretending to be on my side,
Then he told me a massive lie.

Looking for a way out,
I had a massive doubt,
Found a holly and ivy shop,
Decorations climbed to the top.

I walked around
And found a path on the ground,
In front of me was a ginger house,
Running away was a sick little mouse.

Running outside,
I stood and cried,

I will never find a home,
I will be trapped here alone.

Sophie May Taylor (10)
Barley Hill Primary School, Thame

Mermaid Unicorn

M agical powers using every time
E nchanted creature
R eally beautiful hair glowing in the sun
M ysterious eyes that follow you everywhere you go
A mazingly kind to humans
I nteresting behaviour all the time
D eceiving body that you cannot trust

U nusual behaviour when it is angry
N arwhal horn, pricking everyone
I ntelligent brains working hard
C razy posture ready to pounce
O bviously amazing that everyone likes
R esourceful using its poo as skittles
N ever-ending tail, hair dragging on the floor.

Alisha Nicole Thomas (10)
Barley Hill Primary School, Thame

Candy And Unicorn Land

There is a land far, far away
Where if you go you will shout, hooray
A magic land of happiness and fun
It's an incredible place for everyone

There's a sparkly lemonade river
And nothing to make you shiver
There's delicious lollipop trees
With candy cane leaves

Where sweet gingerbread men people walk
And cookie people talk
Where there are glistening gems instead of sand
In the distance there's a unicorn band

At the end of the strawberry lace
There's a chocolate bar castle place
Where unicorns rule
While chilling in a chocolate pool

Sarah Carr (9)
Barley Hill Primary School, Thame

My Day In A Doll's House

I woke up this morning
Feeling rather small,
I sat up in bed
And realised it wasn't my bed at all.

I got up, walking around
And looked in the mirror,
My arms and legs were plastic
And I was much thinner.

I looked in my wardrobe
And saw a dress for a ball,
It glittered in front of my eyes
That must have cost so much at the mall.

I tiptoed down the stairs
With my tiny feet,
I decided I was hungry
And got something to eat.

Suddenly I saw the label
'Barbie' on my cereal,
Wow, I'm in a doll's house!

Lydia Russell (10)
Barley Hill Primary School, Thame

I Wonder

I would like to race in the biggest cars and win every day.
I would like to ride a rocket all day to Mars.
I would like to ride a bike through France.
I would like to ride a train through a volcano.
I would like a trip through galaxies in a UFO and a spaceship.

I wonder if I could fly through the cold wind and skies?
I wonder if I could taste the fluffy clouds?
I wonder if I could meditate in a quiet oasis?
I wonder if I could float like a leaf and be as still as a tree?

I wish I could be a dragon and breathe out money.
I wish I could be a dragon and do anything.

Aleksander Oleksiuk (9)

Barley Hill Primary School, Thame

Underwater Dolphins' Disco

Do you know what dolphins do,
Underneath the waters blue?
Every Friday night they dance,
And don't you know they even prance.

As the sun sets behind the cave,
All the dolphins smile and wave.
They put on their party hats
And start to swim and loudly clap.

In a flash it goes so bright
Oh wait, they turned on the lights,
Seaweed floating all around,
The dolphins making party sounds.

Having a disco under the sea,
The dolphins were looking at me,
Dolphins dancing everywhere,
Enjoying life without a care.

Joslyn Romeril (11)
Barley Hill Primary School, Thame

Living On A Cloud

I felt as small as a koala,
The sun shone like a yellow banana,
The clouds were as soft as wool,
They tasted sweet and sour,
The birds crashed into my castle,
And meeting friends was such a hassle,
I soared through the sky,
With no majestic wings,
I could still see
My castle on a cloud,
It felt sensational,
The wind flying through,
Breathtaking the strong castle gates,
They opened up with no fear to face,
I flew through the sky,
Flowing extremely high,
Since I live a great life
On my castle on a cloud.

Charlotte Watford (10)
Barley Hill Primary School, Thame

Cookie Planet

Somewhere in the galaxy,
Not so far away,
There is a planet made of cookies,
With a beautiful sweet scent.

There is a lake,
Lined with cookies,
A cookie duck swims in it,
Gliding through the water.

Beside the lake there stands
A cookie tree swaying in the breeze,
Every now and then a cookie falls off
And a new one automatically regrows.

The smell of the planet is so sweet
You can smell it from miles away,
When you enter this world
Nothing could ever smell better
Than the cookie planet.

Kelsey Faith Phillips (10)
Barley Hill Primary School, Thame

The Bunny Lasers

I saw a bunny shooting rainbow lasers from
his eyes
as he spun his ears around to fly high into the
skies.

The bunny does anything he wants to do because
he's the boss
so he turns everything into pink fluffy candyfloss.

He sees lots of pink fluffy candyfloss trees.

As much as he loves to eat stuff off the blue
candyfloss planet
he also loves pomegranate.

Whenever the bunny rides rainbows
he turns the colours of a bow.

The bunny also always smells of honey
and he also loves to be funny.

Saskia Keogh (9)
Barley Hill Primary School, Thame

Riding On A Caterpillar Fish

One day I was sailing on my dusty, rusty ship.
I went to the side and got seasick.
A caterpillar fish came up to say hello,
Then I wondered what else could be down below.
"Hey you," I said.
"Can I have a ride down in your seabed?"
"Yeah sure," the caterpillar roared,
I jumped on and saw a shark.
Which came and followed me in the dark,
The caterpillar fish felt oozie woozie.
I jumped off the caterpillar fish
And waved goodbye.
That's my dream,
Maybe next time I could fly!

Brooke Goodchild (10)
Barley Hill Primary School, Thame

Kittens

K ittens are cute, cute as a baby dolphin learning how to swim.

I t was magical, I saw lots of grey tabby kittens strolling across the emerald green, shimmering, beautiful grass.

T hey are adorable, I wish I had a wonderful grey tabby kitten.

T hough I would die to have a unicorn I really want a kitten now I just have to wait until I am twenty-three.

E very time I see a cat or a kitten I scream, "Kitty cat!"

N ow I really, desperately want to go to the amazing pet shop to buy an adorable kitten!

Isabella Kirkwood (9)
Barley Hill Primary School, Thame

The Mysterious Book Of Wisdom And War

It's said there's a magical book,
You'll find it if you really look.
It will surely give you powers,
But only lasts for a few hours.
It will gift you with wisdom and war
But don't be selfish and ask for more.

Somewhere tall,
Within cold halls,
Hides the book
Of wisdom and war.
Look in every open door,
Look closely; you'll find it I'm sure.

It's hidden really well,
If you find it don't tell.
It's between you and me,
It could ruin history.

Mia Nicholls (10)
Barley Hill Primary School, Thame

Land Of Green Talking Mushrooms

Far, far, far away,
The little mushrooms come to play,
Dancing with their evil eye,
Singing along to the sweet tune.

I see a green object,
The mushrooms coming from far away,
I see their clown pose,
And their sweet smile,
They will come play again.

I step out of Wonderland,
To see the real world,
Trees, birds and nature
But no mushrooms.

From that day on I dream of them,
So soft just like a feather,
I hope to see this place again,
But was it just a wonder?

Olivia Pitts (11)
Barley Hill Primary School, Thame

The Funfair Madness

For one night only for me and my friends,
With roller coasters that loop the loop,
And haunted houses that scare you to death.
Also, don't forget food and drink stands that cost nothing.
A giant beach with a huge diner in the middle,
Where anyone can go and eat their food.
Also the dodgems, don't forget them,
It's not like you will pay to go on.
As I look around I can spot people's faces
After exiting the haunted houses,
And I can also hear some people screaming on the roller coaster.

Theo Newitt (10)
Barley Hill Primary School, Thame

Mofi's Sugar Rush World

Mofi is my pet,
And he is the best pet yet,
Mofi is very cheeky
But when he is tired he is very peaky.

He is not very smart
And he has a big heart.

He ate too many sweets
And it was a big treat.

Mofi felt sick so he had to stop for a break
But I thought it was fake.

He went to bed
Because he bumped his head.
He went to Candy Crush,
Which made him have a sugar rush.
In a world of treats and sweets
The world finishes and then comes the fishes.

Ellie Rose Boswell (10)
Barley Hill Primary School, Thame

Playing Football Inside A Volcano

As a helicopter drops him in
He wonders, *let's go play some football*
But just as he did lava people came out.

They looked like natives of a volcano
They had lava skin
But they challenged him to a football game.

For the game they accepted it
They shook like a hook
And didn't let go.

He held his hand
As tight as could be
He started but wanted it to end.

He started as quick as possible,
He scored three, they scored one,
He had won!

Jack Masterson (10)
Barley Hill Primary School, Thame

The Unicorn House

I walked into that beautiful world.
Candy canes by my side
That sweet-smelling scent,
Nothing could be better.
Those pine, candy trees,
As I put my arm out,
Brushing my hands against it.

My feet on the candy grass
Tickling my ankle.
A glimpse caught my eyes,
A beautiful fluffy house,
White with a pink mane,
Two eyes like a window
And a mouth as a door,
A horn as a chimney,
As golden as can be.
Nothing could be better,
Than the unicorn house.

Freya Dodd (10)
Barley Hill Primary School, Thame

The Cheesy Trampoline

A trampoline that can jump you to the moon.
Past the gloom to the bright cheesy moon,
Frying the moon to eat on toast is really absurd,
If you are higher than a bird,
Waving to every rocket in sight
But being careful everything doesn't fly out your pocket,
Seeing a shooting star,
Shut your eyes and make a wish...
I wish I could go back to the house and go to bed.
But when I open my eyes
I find out I am already in bed
And notice it was just a dream... or was it?

Mia Heard (9)
Barley Hill Primary School, Thame

An Alligator's Best Friend

The day I fell over the railing,
I thought that my life was going to be failing
I didn't know that was happening,
Until I met a mysterious creature.

A new start, a new beginning,
We slept next to each other,
We played loads of games
But I only liked it when I was winning,
We swam in the water,
I felt like a lamb to the slaughter.

He was getting very naughty,
Each day when he was forty,
He fell asleep,
Sorry I only gave you a peep.

Shanae Abi Martins (10)
Barley Hill Primary School, Thame

Flying High

If I could fly
I would go anywhere,
Everyone would be staring
But I would not care.

I would go so high
The sky behind
I would go anywhere
And the things I would see...

I would see everything,
The wind would howl in my ears,
I would be on top of the world
And I would have no fears.

I would see Italy and Rome,
And Portugal and Spain!
I would see everything
And my amazement would always gain.

If I could fly.

Ava Stevenson (10)
Barley Hill Primary School, Thame

Mark The Shark

Once I saw a shark
His name was Mark
He was blue like the sea
So don't be mean

He's so friendly trust me
You'll find him in Coral Lane
Next to the lion's mane
Mark's friends are really friendly

Then he saw a cave
He swam inside
Ready for an adventure
When he saw the treasure

One day he had a crazy idea
To find Flames, the lava shark
He set off to find him
When he saw the humans about to flip.

Thomas Bates (9)
Barley Hill Primary School, Thame

The Flight

The majestic beast has blood-red scales,
As smooth as a white sea pearl,
Huge dark red wings flap through the night,
She has bright green eyes which shine in the sky.

When you get on this creature,
You will feel a tingle in your spine,
In the air the ride is smooth
And you feel safe and secure.

On my adventure, I went to many places,
Wonders of the world, famous cities,
Beautiful images stuck in my head,
When flying around on my dragon.

Olie Grubb (10)
Barley Hill Primary School, Thame

The Land Of The Talking Cookies

Cookies living differently,
Some floating into space,
Candy canes and candy lanes,
With sweets falling constantly,
A waterfall that never stops flowing.

Cookies eating unicorn poop,
Living on Waterdiddlemelon Island,
Hear the gushing of the waterfall,
With cookie crumbs covering the floor.

The kids' cookies go down the river,
Since they think it's a slide,
They have so much fun,
But their mothers cry, "Get down!"

Chloe Chamberlain (11)
Barley Hill Primary School, Thame

Lollipop Land

I am a delicious, nutritious lollipop
Who eats melted pops
I live in a lollipop house
Next to the lake
It's ooey, it's gooey
The lollipops are yummy in my tummy.

I got a delicious gummy
It was super yummy
No one eats healthy foods
You only eat lolly foods.

If you eat cucumber or tomatoes
You aren't in luck
You don't tuck in
For things that are yuck
You are in jail
"Ha ha!" said the kale.

Ruby Ford (9)
Barley Hill Primary School, Thame

Sea And Lava

A shark that is crazy
His name is Sharpedo
He wears blue armour
Terrifying creature

He once rode a lightning bolt
He made it turn into a rainbow
His armour is made of ice
It gives him powers to breathe ice and snow

Sharpedo once had an idea
To swim in lava
He saw a lava shark
They became friends

The lava shark's name is Flame
He wears red armour
Flame lives in a volcano
Best friends till the end.

Jake Rigby (9)
Barley Hill Primary School, Thame

Having A Pig Ride!

I started to fly with a pig that went super high,
I brought a shiny tie in a yucky, sticky pie,
The pig tried the mushy, disgusting pie,
A funny cow rode a colourful bike in the blue sky,
For just a second, the pig looked shy,
It was so spectacular I began to cry.

The pig was so kind,
That I had a smile for a long time,
I had to go down because I was too high,
The shy pig stole the yucky pie,
I didn't mind that he stole the yucky pie.

Toby Dodd (7)
Barley Hill Primary School, Thame

Gary The Giant

Riding a giant
Riding through town
It is so fun
I'm eating a bun
His name is Gary
He's friends with Barry
He had a baby called Harry.

Captain Red is ready for adventure
On a quest to find the best treasure.
He has blue eyes and blonde hair
He loves to eat burgers on the ship.

This is a land far, far away
With mysterious creatures on their way
They are soft and fluffy
They do feel like my beard.

Jacob Alexander Ellis (9)
Barley Hill Primary School, Thame

The Cupcake

Once there lived an old man and a broom
Now this old man was magic
And his broomstick was the magic
One day he was hungry for a cupcake
But not any normal cupcake
A different cupcake with a weird flavour
So he turned his broomstick round and round
And cast the spell
Then *boom!* A giant cupcake appeared in his sight
A broccoli and duck cupcake with baby food frosting
And cabbage sparkles with a Brussel as a cherry.

Lois Mae Rowark (10)
Barley Hill Primary School, Thame

The Flying Unicorn

I saw the most silliest-billyest unicorn,
flying in the air.
I saw the unicorn doing loop-the-loops,
it was a crazy and lazy idea,
and it was very silly and I thought his name was
Silly Billy!
No one believed me, everyone denied it,
but it was a disgraceful place to be.
No one would see me and Billy,
and there was a baby stuck onto his back,
with Blu Tack!
But it was very stupid tack, because it untacked!

Asa Varnam (7)
Barley Hill Primary School, Thame

The Key To Time, Shape And Place

The magic necklace shimmering in the sun,
Waiting for that lucky person to have some fun,
Jack bent down to pick it up,
A green gem shone and flashed light,
Took the key out and played with it,
He looked at the gem with his magnifying kit.

He took the key out
And had a play about,
The necklace was full of wonder,
He put it on and heard thunder,
He pulled at the key
And he was full of glee.

Tyron Alex Johnson (10)
Barley Hill Primary School, Thame

Friends In A Forest

Camping outside in an adventurous world.
Cooking melting marshmallows on a fire.
Flickering flames dance swiftly.

Sleeping bags all snug and warm.
Stars light the sky.
Twinkling so bright with all their might.
In a tent with my friends.
Lots of fun to be had.

Camping in a forest.
What excitement!
Was that a unicorn flying free, flying fast?
I'm sure it was!
Can it be?

Libby Elton (9)
Barley Hill Primary School, Thame

Underwater Dolphin Disco

Do you know what dolphins do
Underneath the water blue?
Every Friday night they dance
And don't you know, they even prance.

When the sun sets over the sea
The dolphins come out to play,
In a flash they make a splash,
Because they are ready to have some fun.

The party began in a hurry,
But one of them was in a scurry,
After being chased by a shark,
Everyone left their mark.

Holly Mitchell (11)
Barley Hill Primary School, Thame

The Rapping, Dancing Pug

I am a pug, my name is Jay.
I like to dance in the rain.
When it rains I am down the lane
Saying my rap and shaking my chain.
Others may think I am a pain
For dancing, singing and rapping away.

They may say, "Stop!"
But I want to shine like a star in the night sky.
I try to shine night and day
And dance the night away.
Then I shout, "Rain, come another day!"

Leah Butler (10)
Barley Hill Primary School, Thame

Underwater Life

U nusual
N avy blue
D iving underwater
E xcellent experience
R iding on my blown-up doughnut
W et as a working washing machine
A cold night
T urquoise water
E xtra cleaning
R ubbish when you eat

L ight underwater
I n the warm water
F ly through the water when I swim
E xciting.

Summer Lily Evans (10)
Barley Hill Primary School, Thame

Sparklessourswinselpop Land

As I walked through the door,
My eyes opened to candy galore,
Sour laces, giant lollipops,
I was in Heaven,
Sweet bubblegum air and rainbow waterfalls,
In the corner of my eye I saw a marshmallow ball.
I wanted to eat it all but I didn't know where to start.
The next thing I saw was a love dart, it was Cupid.
I turned my eye to a majestic unicorn
Could this day get any better?

Ellen Lucy Marriner (10)

Barley Hill Primary School, Thame

Land Of The Talking Toilets

Hello, we are the talking toilets
Our king is the biggest toilet of them all.
If you don't know that then you'll be a fool.

I am your imagination,
Think too hard and I will be your creation.

The toilets inside are very nice
But sometimes there's a bit of spice.

If you mess with us
We will flush you down
And then we will claim our big brown crown!

Sam Davison (10) & Volke

Barley Hill Primary School, Thame

The Fireball's Feelings

I am a little fireball,
Little, cute and warm.
A magical memory,
Can roll on water,
The water of imagination and magic.

Suddenly I see land
And lots of sand,
Trees and leaves,
Homes of many people,
Wooden and warm.

All alone and sad,
Little ball of fire,
Rolled back on the water,
Nice and warm back at home,
Nice and quiet,
Go to bed.

Riley Farrell (9)
Barley Hill Primary School, Thame

My Vampire Friend, Amy

I went to visit my friend,
Her house feels cold,
She is very old,
Sometimes scary but never hairy,
She hates water but is full of laughter.

The yellow sun is very rum,
She wears her daylight ring in case of the sun,
She is my best friend
Although she does sometimes put on a show,
She isn't very good at punctuation,
What does Amy need?
A capital letter!

Lola Brown (10)
Barley Hill Primary School, Thame

When I Woke Up

When I woke up in the morning,
In my old bed, yawning,
My bed seemed bigger
Than any day before.

I tried to move around and roll,
But it was as if I was in a bowl,
I was the size of a bee,
I tried to get up but it was a big deed.

I then saw the trouble ahead,
A big, hairy spider in my bed,
I suddenly realised I was dreaming
And I woke up beaming.

Justin Constantine Grimes (11)
Barley Hill Primary School, Thame

I Can Fly!

As I looked in the mirror
I thought to myself, *I can fly!*

Next time I stood up high on the hill
I looked down and wondered, *why oh why?*

I am no bird, I am no plane,
I haven't got any feathers or wings.

I am a nine-year-old girl
With a wild imagination.

Could I let this get to me
Or do I need to do some meditation?

Rose Macbeth-Benson (9)
Barley Hill Primary School, Thame

Food

Bacon bubbling,
Sausages sizzling,
Muffins moaning,
French fries frizzling.

A marshmallow dancing to the cello,
Burgers bumping,
Spaghetti slopping,
Hot dogs jumping.

Cheerios cheering,
Shreddies shredding,
Frosties frosting,
Great big chickens doing the bedding.

Aero, KitKat, Snickers, Mars,
Yorkie, Twix and Milkybars!

Ben Barrie (9)
Barley Hill Primary School, Thame

Candy Crisis

I created a portal,
As a play,
I became immortal,
And went away.

In a different land,
I looked around,
And felt some candy in my hand.

I walked for days,
And began to shout,
In the candy blaze,
No one was about.

I came across a shop,
And found a portal,
Stepped through and fell down a drop.

Kirsty Cleare (11)
Barley Hill Primary School, Thame

Runaway Burger

Toasted bun, with a finger gun,
Next was the cheese, chatting to the peas,
After was the lettuce and then the tomatoes.
And of course, the patty, looking like a fatty.
Next was the chips, running from the dips.
It all came together making a burger monster!
Running away from me, spraying lots of mustard,
Looking like jets of custard.

Dylan Georgiou-White (10)
Barley Hill Primary School, Thame

Food Rush

When I woke up
I had my Cheerios,
It's really nice,
Apparently, it tasted like rice!

Then Dad got baking
Some bacon and sausages,
But then he baked some egg
And then the egg went on my leg.

So then I had some delicious bacon
And then I had a little play,
But before lunch
I had a little munch!

Joshua Lewis (9)
Barley Hill Primary School, Thame

Underwater Disco

Do you know what dolphins do at night?
They have a party.
They dance and prance.
They have a wonderful night.
They invite all the other animals.
Blue and beautiful the sea shines.
The sharks have squid for dinner.
The dolphins have fish for dinner.
The fish have tadpoles for dinner.
They have tables with cloths.

Caelyn Ferreira (9)
Barley Hill Primary School, Thame

The Girl And The Flying Dog's Adventures

One fine day I was thinking,
Sitting all alone
But not for long...

A flying dog
Flew into my home.

I climbed upon his back,
It was as soft as silk.

Whoosh!
Quickly, out the window
We both flew away
To a land far away.

To the Cupcake Land
That made our day.

Katie Mace (9)
Barley Hill Primary School, Thame

Untitled

On my meteor lived a crazy mouse
He lived in a tasty hot dog house
One morning he heard a sound
And ran fast outside his house
He saw a big fat mouse
And his name was Klaus
Klaus nibbled on his house
The crazy mouse cried,
"Klaus, stop it!
It's my house,
You have your own house!"

Calvin Schuman (9)
Barley Hill Primary School, Thame

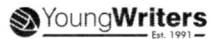

The Land Of Sports And Gaming

Football is a sport,
Sports can be football,
This place is for sports,
As well as gaming.

Today is the day to kick-off,
Let's try to get no one sent off,
Let's go for a 10m swim,
Now let's go for a game,
We'll go do it for fun not fame.
3, 2, 1... Kick, kick!

Finlay Ryan (10)
Barley Hill Primary School, Thame

My Giant Pickle

Polishing his rotten teeth
I got my arm right underneath.
I saw bits of his leftover meals
And the treats he steals.

When I bent down
His mouth closed shut
And now I have teeth marks in my butt!
Never go near his tonic water
Because if you do then you'll be slaughtered!

Róisín Caldwell (10)
Barley Hill Primary School, Thame

Witch School

The witches rocket around the sky.
They fly, fly, fly.
The witches' cat is very black,
It's black, black, black!

The witches' spells float around the moon,
They zoom, zoom, zoom!
The witch's nose is more disgusting than her toes,
Her toes, toes, toes!

Elodie Varnam (9)
Barley Hill Primary School, Thame

Rocky Moon Battles

The asteroids raced down like a rocket
Zooming from planet to planet
As somebody flying.

Pokémon and heroes flying over and under planets
Like a dolphin jumping up and down in the water.

Battling and being masterly
To take over to the end like a video game.

Kris Toft (9)
Barley Hill Primary School, Thame

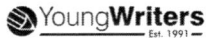

Weather

The rain shoots down like a fast car.
The rain is fluffy like a squishy cloud.
It runs across the pipe like something in a race.

The rain made lakes and rivers in a click of a
finger.
The rain made the grass shoot up like a bullet.
People putting humongous raincoats on.

Kai Green (9)
Barley Hill Primary School, Thame

World Of Wolves

A muddy, disgusting planet where wolves can talk.
Orange trees and horrible manners.
This is the place where wolves can be themselves
Like killing their own prey.
Beautiful grey wolves only live here.
If any humans come they will be dead in three
seconds.

Grace Clark (10)

Barley Hill Primary School, Thame

What A Wonderful World It Is

In my eyes the world seems like a butterfly
fluttering above the sky.
It seems like my place when I stare into space
And see what a wonderful world it is.

I jumped off a cloud and I screamed aloud,
"What a wonderful world it is,
Oh wow, what a wonderful world it is!"

On this planet, I sit with my family,
Feeling love as I stared at the stars above
And I think to myself, *I love my world.*

Below me I see a lollipop tree, glittering in the sun.
It seemed like fun, when I climbed to the sun
And thought to myself, *what a wonderful world.*

I felt magic inside, when I ran and cried,
"What a wonderful world it is,
Oh wow, what a wonderful world it is."

My love was so strong, I stumbled along,
Rolling down a hill and I thought to myself,
What a wonderful world,
Oh wow, what a wonderful world.

Georgia Wright (8)

Chandlings School, Kennington

Pet Dragon

I have a pet dragon, he is very nice indeed.
The only strange thing is he thinks the pet is me.
He feeds me my favourite popcorn sprinkle.
He strokes me with his tail.
Although it is quite spiky
We play fetch.
My dragon throws the burger
And I run in the opposite direction.
He gave me a name.
My dragon trains me to sit, roll and handstand.
If I am bad my dragon nibbles me with a little tooth.
He takes me to the vet
And then to bed for some rest.
We go for walks past the clouds
He and me have tea and gummies.
We dress up in hats and dresses for parties.
We are next-door neighbours.
It seems so far away.
We jump in icing puddles and slide down tree trunks.

We buy lots of things like rocket hats and lily pads.
I have a pet dragon, he is very nice indeed.
The only strange thing is he thinks the pet is me.

Sophia Stewart (8)
Chandlings School, Kennington

A Running Burger

"These mouths are bad!"
First to my friends those mouths said
"How beautiful and cute they are!"
But then they ate them.
"Those chairs are worse because on them our
killers sit.
Tables are the worst because on those we are
killed."
So now I want to run
I am put on the plate and onto the table
Now the mouth is opening and wants to eat me
Suddenly I run through the restaurant
And the mouth is behind me
I see how other mouths kill hot dogs, vanilla ice
creams,
Biscuits, beans, crisps and other burgers
But I am running
Luckily for me the door of the restaurant is open.
I am away from those humans!

Anastasiya Sinitsina (7)
Chandlings School, Kennington

Food Breeds Of Birds

Doughnut parrots, flying free,
Singing wildly, saying 'he he he',
Honey parrots sitting in trees,
Trying to get rid of their fleas.

Lemon robins eating their food,
Having a chat about the macaws with a mood,
Pepper robins getting into their house
And hearing a tiny mouse.

Chocolate toucans drinking syrup,
Cleaning their stirrup,
Squishy toucans watering flowers,
Getting rid of slug showers.

Peach pigeons skipping around,
Shaking hands and being proud,
Jam pigeons nibbling nuts,
Saying tut, tut, tut!

Now it is time for them all to go to bed.

Emmeline Pink (8)
Chandlings School, Kennington

The Giant Donkey Smelling Potatoes Dancing

I was born from rigid potatoes,
They were even crazier than flying tomatoes.
I had only one small choice to make,
And that was only to jump into a lake!
I screamed, "Argh!"
Then I shrieked, "Ooohh arr!"
And I freaked frantically,
The giant dancing potatoes had giant ears!
I was trying to flee,
But there were just too many.
They were so flexible
And just so, so funny,
I really could not resist laughing out loud,
It was just way too weirdly mad!
I screamed, "Ha, ha, ha!"
To my mum's potato's dad,
He had a hairy, fake moustache!

Sofia Trajtenberg (8)
Chandlings School, Kennington

What A Wacky World

I've landed on the moon holding a balloon,
Now I'm on the sun eating a hot dog bun.
I've landed on Mars but there were no more gold
bars.
An ogre wants to play tennis with me
But I can't, I might be late for tea.
Now I don't know what to do
Because I really need the loo!
My rocket is weird for it has a beard.
I'm in Sunningwell and I made friends with a cow
who rings a bell.
I'm on a boat with the three billy goats.
Swimming in the River Nile, being chased by a
crocodile.
It's sad because for 365 days a year I can't drink
any more beer!

Louis Isaacs (8)
Chandlings School, Kennington

The Sweet Shop

The sweet shop is one million billion storeys tall,
Filled with trillions of sweets,
So many delicious ones to decide from,
Which ones shall I take?

Should I take a gobstopper
Or should I have a Fanged Finger Friend that lasts
for a year?
Or should I take a Caramel Delight Deluxe?

Which one should I take?
So many to decide from.
They say that the Frisbee Friends Deluxe are the
best
But are they?
Should I try them?
You decide.
My choice is to try all of them.
What's your favourite?

Arnav Jain (8)
Chandlings School, Kennington

I Had Tea With A Penguin

I had tea with a penguin on top of a building,
A building, I know it sounds funny,
But it didn't go very well.
First the carpet flew away
Then the leaves flew on my face,
But then with luck the carpet flew back.
So we flew back like a genie
So we went on the sofa all cuddled up
And also under a blanket.
I watched a film, the film was absolutely cool,
It had lots of things like superheroes,
Enemies and also animals,
Such things like cats, dogs and horses.
But after a while we both fell fast asleep.

Martha Payne (7)
Chandlings School, Kennington

The Edible Planet

Ellie flew through the sky
And landed with a cry,
Ellie was on something wobbly,
Was it jelly?
She jumped off the jelly with her belly
And walked over to a chocolate fountain,
The fountain looked all glittery,
Ellie looked over to a mountain.

She then looked up and saw a bowl of coffee,
But then she said, "No, I prefer toffee!"
Then she tasted something bitter,
Now she could see lots of litter!
She gobbled up a scoop of ice cream,
Ellie woke up and realised this was all a dream!

Olivia Arbuckle (8)
Chandlings School, Kennington

Ice Skating Dinosaurs

One day I looked out of my window
And saw ice skating dinosaurs.
They slipped and got up
And then they fell over again.
I went outside and they just kept going and going
So I had to go, it was so slippery.
The dinos were angry and cold.
Their scales were sharp and pointy
And their breath stank of rotten fish and deer.
One of the dinos had fallen into some water
When he got out he was covered in ice and water.
He was rampaging around the lake.
Suddenly all the ice broke and everyone fell in.

Thomas Liddiard (8)
Chandlings School, Kennington

The Golden Lightning Bolt

Lying in my bed dreaming of lightning bolts and
stars.
Suddenly the magic key started glowing,
And I got lifted into my dream and woke up.
As soon as I woke up, *zoom!*
A lightning bolt brought me up into the
shimmering night sky.
The lightning bolt suddenly talked!
It said, "I will kill you if you don't get off my back!"
You could tell that the lightning bolt was angry
So I jumped off the lightning bolt
And landed in my bed.
I never knew what happened nor did anyone else.

Charlotte Carter (8)

Chandlings School, Kennington

Dino Dinner

I had an unexpected call
From a tall, scary dinosaur.
He wanted to come over at dinner time
And I told him it was a roast with thyme.
He said that that would be great
And suddenly smashed through the gate.
He came in and crushed the chair
So I had to go get a spare.
The food went everywhere,
Up the walls and in my hair.
The gravy went up my nose,
He threw the broccoli down his clothes.
I can't believe the mess he made,
I would give him an 'F' grade.

Andy Chengchao Xu (9)
Chandlings School, Kennington

The Magic Bus

One day I saw a bus, it didn't look like other buses,
Instead it had a stick sticking out of its roof
And instead of being green it was bright red.
When I hopped onboard it really was a trip.
Suddenly it started to move.
The next thing I knew I was in outer space.
With an almighty creak the doors opened wide.
I floated out but soon the bus called me back
And in no time at all we were back.
The next day I hopped aboard again.
I wondered where we'd go...

Kiyan Irani (7)
Chandlings School, Kennington

A Planet Over There

I know a planet over there
Full of china cats.
Cats from every corner.

Ping! went a china vase
As the cats came through.
Dancing, laughing, swirling, twirling,
Tumbling, whirling, running and chasing.

Cats of all types of colours and sizes.
Ginger, tabby, pink, blue, black, white,
Even neon green!

I wish I could go there to the planet
Swarming with cats,
Such a wonderful place,
I love it so!

Arianna Malmberg (8)
Chandlings School, Kennington

Underwater Farm

Underwater I heard squeaks and squirms
As I go down the strange noises get louder and louder.
Then suddenly I see the strangest sight in the world,
An underwater farm.
A farm with pigs that squirm
And ducks that squeak.
Horses that say miaow
And cats that say neigh.
I have found a strange sight indeed,
A sight that squirms,
A sight that squeaks, miaows and neighs.
A sight with pigs and horses.
A sight I may never see again.

Helena Fleming (8)
Chandlings School, Kennington

Horse Riding Underwater

I came through the magic door
Admiring what was at the other side
First I saw I was in crystal-clear water
With a whiff, I smelt some candy
I thought, *where must I be?*
I walked over to a girl with a weird purple octopus head.
I saw some horses and the girl pointed at them.
When I was on the horse I was speechless,
It was mental.
With a click of someone's hand
I was in my dusty bed in a soaking wet suit!

Chloé Paulus (8)
Chandlings School, Kennington

The Day I Met A Talking Clock

It was just a normal day
So I went to the café.
I sat on a stool and ordered some tea
Then I looked at the clock
And couldn't believe what I could see!
A clock with eyes and a mouth too
Just as I was getting over my shock
The clock started to speak
It sounded like a door that had never been oiled
It said with a squeak,
"Ah! Blackcurrant tea, my favourite!"

Freya Osborne (8)
Chandlings School, Kennington

I Was Bitten

I liked lizards
The green and soft skin
Then one bit me!
Now I am not so keen.
I liked dogs
The soft fur and crazy play
Then one bit me
Now I keep away.
I liked hamsters
So cute and small
Then one bit me
Now I don't like them at all.
I now like penguins
Their waddle and water flight
But best of all, absolutely no bite!

James Lee (7)
Chandlings School, Kennington

Hot Tub Time Machine

I jumped in the tub ready for a scrub,
The water turned green, I gave a scream.
The bubbles churned and my stomach turned,
I landed in a shallow pool next to a ruler of Gaul,
A Roman came along and told me to go to the
baths,
So I jumped in the first one,
The water turned green, I yelled, "Woohoo!"
Then I went forward in time and then went to bed.

Jasper James Bromage (8)
Chandlings School, Kennington

The Magic Sea

Mermaids swim through the clear sea
Fish dart in and out of seaweed
In the magic sea

Dolphins play near the sea bay
Otters float about
In the magic sea

Ships sail on the sea above
While sharks lurk below
In the magic sea

Crabs scuttle about on the rocky seabed
Octopuses hide, hoping to catch a fish
In the magic sea.

Xanthe Hodgin (8)
Chandlings School, Kennington

Fish Servant

There once was a fish
That served people with a dish
He is a servant to the king
That wears lots of bling
He worked day and night
But once got into a fight
He brought the king the wrong food
He found it very rude
He didn't listen to the royal
But he wasn't very loyal
The king wanted some ham
But instead he brought him a lamb.

Max Cavaliere (9)
Chandlings School, Kennington

The Cookie Moon

As I stood on the cookie moon
I saw a zebra holding a spoon
But this zebra was not normal
And besides, it was a portal
The zebra was blue and yellow
I was hoping it was quite mellow
I walked over to it
It looked like it was having a fit
Its face was grumpy
Its body was lumpy
And then, *bang!*
It turned into a venomous fang!

Rufus Worrall (7)
Chandlings School, Kennington

Monsters On The Moon

M onsters' crew flying to the moon.
O n the moon they find a spoon.
N eeding food they begin to hunt.
S uddenly on the hunt they begin to grump.
T o the lagoon they go.
E nding up just finding snow.
R ubbish this moon place, they thought.
S o let's get back with what we have caught.

Evie Jefferis (7)
Chandlings School, Kennington

Touch The Ground Dead

Die if you touch the ground,
If you touch the ground you're dead.
You'll be sent straight to bed,
You can smell a bin that is very weird,
And I can hear nothing at all.
If you touch the ground you're dead,
You need to get it into your head.
This game is not just for fun,
Please don't go telling your mom!

Max Lucking (7)
Chandlings School, Kennington

Evil Clocks Around The World

One day there was a school with evil clocks in it
The evil clocks were mischievous
You don't want to see it.
They didn't look evil
They looked you over.
If you see one with sharp teeth and a face, get out!
Because it has sharp laser eyes and it could kill you.
So if you see them remember,
Get out of the room!

Archie Warrilow (8)
Chandlings School, Kennington

Candy Land

In a land full of sweets, with candy for streets
And cute dragons for pets.
Flake and candyfloss trees
With honey made by bees
And furry cookies for carpets!
Someone found toffee inside their coffee
And jelly for a house!
People turn purple
And feel like a turtle
With their dragons bringing them candy!

Jaya R S Hill (7)
Chandlings School, Kennington

Mr Boyle

M r Boyle, jumping out of the window
R unning down the corridor go the children

B oiling eggs and throwing them all over
O ily sausages growing out of his ears
Y oung children running everywhere
L earning children no more
E llie had the best day ever.

Ellie May Bromley (7)
Chandlings School, Kennington

The Mermaid

M usic, music, it made me fall.
E ven though I love music and I transformed
R ing, ring! went my phone
M y new power had arrived. I froze it
A nd then
I climbed out of the sea but my
D ad came so I climbed back in until he had gone
then I got out again.

Alice Carol Rendell (7)
Chandlings School, Kennington

Surfing The Sun

In the air
Like a giant bear

I flew to the top of the sun
On a giant balloon

To surf the sun
As everyone thought it was a pun!

Bubbling lava
Flying asteroids

Rocks on fire
Filled with smoke

Sun was furious
While I melted into the heat.

Anur Nayak (8)
Chandlings School, Kennington

Underwater Skating

I hear the swish of the waves above.
I see the crystal-clear water on my body.
I feel the warm hand of the mermaid.
The mermaid has a pink and turquoise fish-scaled tail.
My roller skates are neon yellow, sparkling in the sea water.
Our hair was like octopus legs, swishing in the sea.

Pratiba Stewart (8)
Chandlings School, Kennington

Ninjas And Dragons

Ninjas riding an invisible dragon
they were flying in the sky,
soaring beautifully way up high.
Invisible dragons flying through a portal,
they must have felt pretty immortal.
"Never come down," they began to sing,
until they heard the dinner bell ring.

Stella De Silva (7)
Chandlings School, Kennington

The Circus

I went to the circus
And guess what I saw?

A fat elephant doing the trapeze.
Amazingly it did it with ease.
But suddenly it spotted a mouse,
It wanted to cry and run to its house.
It let go of the bar
And landed on the ringmaster!

Uh-oh!

Holly Andrews (7)
Chandlings School, Kennington

Skittles Go Mad

Skittles jumping out of the bag
Kicking and pushing to the top
I ran away in despair
They chased me and chased me
They don't eat
They pulled me down to the ground
"Lick me!" they cried
"Urgh!" Freddie replied
Skittles denied.

Freddie Anders (7)
Chandlings School, Kennington

Speak With A Dog

I'm excited to have a dog that talks.
And says he loves to go on walks.
He tells me that he likes goats cheese.
But he should have said 'please'.
My dog asks to play ball
So he made a telephone call.
And I said, "You are an amazing dog."

Felix Grund (8)
Chandlings School, Kennington

The Singing Cheese

I wish there was a singing cheese
But wait, over there in the sun
Lots of different ones, singing in a choir!
But then I notice it is a cheese,
Not just any cheese but a golden cheese
But then there appear to be lots of cheeses
Singing right there!

Sid Davies (8)
Chandlings School, Kennington

The Talking Marshmallow

There was once a talking marshmallow
Who decided to play the cello
And he went to the beach
And played a big screech
So then he shouted below!
Then the talking marshmallow saw all his friends
And what did he do?
He played a big screech!

Laurence Maggs (7)
Chandlings School, Kennington

The Flying Whale

When I came out I saw a flying whale.
"How come?"
I zoomed to my boat to sail.
A guy came and threw me to the cars
Like it's wonderland I cooked the stars.
I even cooked rainbow shrimps with wings
With shell onion rings.

Claire Voillemont-Choi (9)
Chandlings School, Kennington

Goblin On A Quad Bike

There was a goblin
Called Scott Joplin
Who rode a quad bike
In the middle of the night.

One day he ran out of fuel
While he was going to school
He got off his bike
And ran for his life
From the beastly firefly.

Ajeet Nagi (8)
Chandlings School, Kennington

Surf Shark

S urfing
U nder the waves
R olling
F rom side to side

S wimming
H appily in the water
A ttacking a rat that
R elaxes in the sand
K iller surfing shark.

Lara Galvani-Silva (8)
Chandlings School, Kennington

Dinosaur

Once there was a dinosaur that farted
A carrot flew out of his bum
It was scary and made me jump
"I never knew you could make such a loud trump!"
The smell was absolutely horrid,
The mess he made was torrid!

Josh (7)
Chandlings School, Kennington

My Pet JoJo

I have a pet turtle,
His name is JoJo.
In the morning he loves a little cocoa
Then he's ready to go-go!

JoJo loves to race
But he is too slow, slow,
He has a bath
And starts to glow, glow!

Owais Faruq (9)
Chandlings School, Kennington

The Chocolate And Ice Cream Dream

Chocolate falling from the sky
Ice cream mountains everywhere
Chocolate running down the valley
Fluffy marshmallows floating by
Multicoloured sprinkles fluttering
Onto the mounds of my favourite dream.

Zara Hartwright (8)
Chandlings School, Kennington

Sandwiches Eating You

If you see a sandwich nearby
You might want to run as 'they' love to eat you.
The sandwiches are angry!
The sandwiches are nasty!
The sandwiches get eaten.
Hooray, the village was saved!

Jonny Hook (7)
Chandlings School, Kennington

The Fire Unicorn

M outh that blows fire
A tail made out of candy
G lows in water
I can't believe I've seen one
C lever little fire unicorn.

Ellie Thorburn (8)
Chandlings School, Kennington

Lolly Trees

In my dream
Lollipops would grow on trees
Chocolate balls on the breeze
Sugar snow floating about
"Sweets, sweets!"
I want to shout!

Belle White (7)
Chandlings School, Kennington

Purple Pony

Purple pony
Pooping pink poo
Pony, please pick it up
Or use the loo!

Isabella Ferrarese (7)
Chandlings School, Kennington

Peter Pan's Secret

As he sat down and opened the book
Out of the book came a mysterious hook
It said, "Come with me, to Neverland,
Don't be afraid, just take my hand."

Words flew around him like a hurricane blowing,
He stood in awe, not a clue where he was going.
All of a sudden they reached Neverland,
And with a thud, they landed on the sand.

"Come on fairies, come over here,
Can you tell me if there's a toilet near?"
"But Cap'n, I thought you wanted to make this boy
fly?"
"Ah yes, of course!" And they flew into the night
sky.

That's the story of Peter Pan,
Before everyone was a loving fan.
But remember to look out your window each night,
Because you may just glimpse a young boy in
flight!

Hollie Colverson (10)
Great Milton CE Primary School, Oxford

The Castle On The Cloud

The harsh bitter wind howled in my face,
It felt like this was such a horrible place.
Squelch! went my feet as I trudged through the cloud,
Then I suddenly stopped when I heard a strange sound...

It sounded like people, talking from far away.
As I took a big step the clouds started to sway.
Then the howling wind stopped and I looked all around,
People materialised and I suddenly found
A humongous red castle, with a towering red door.
As I stared in amazement I heard a gruff roar,
"Welcome to my castle," I heard the voice say,
"Thank you for coming from so far away."
Then all of a sudden I woke up in my bed,
Was it really a dream? I thought in my head.

Eva Lily Thatcher (10)
Great Milton CE Primary School, Oxford

Battle Of The Birds

What will be the score today?
Tottenham home and Liverpool away.
Liverpool start with three up top,
The obvious choice from Jürgen Klopp.
van Dijk, the leader at the back,
If he plays well, we'll have a crack.
Wijnaldum scores, the crowd goes crazy,
Tottenham's defence are very lazy!
Firmino scores and it's Liverpool's day,
Now Tottenham have a price to pay.
The game's almost over, it's Tottenham's last bet,
Lamela comes on and hits the net.
Is it too late? There's just seconds to go,
Unfortunately not, the game ends with a blow!
The Reds win the game and are top of the pile,
And Jürgen Klopp's day ends with a victorious
smile.

Charlie Morgan Lewis Groves (10)
Great Milton CE Primary School, Oxford

Loch Ness Monster

Is it a girl or is it a boy?
Are there five, six or seven, ahoy?
A ship sails along the coast of Loch Ness
But there's no sound.
There's one thing for sure, it cannot be found
I think it's a girl with eyelashes so long
But try not to blink because in a flash she'll be gone
Her name is Nessie but I like Kelpie, I do
So, I would change it if I were you
Can anyone tell if she's a myth or not?
My family can certainly tell (not)
She lives 800ft down
But she's not that silly as a clown
For a human that's too far down
She likes it private in her own little town.

Esmée Webb (10)
Great Milton CE Primary School, Oxford

Alice In Wonderland

Our story begins in a meadow when the sun was
shining brightly.
Alice was sitting quietly as her sister read.
Suddenly she saw a white furry head.
Alice crept behind him until they reached a hole.
Down the hole she jumped, will this ever end?
Round the corners until she reached a door.
She found a little bottle which said 'drink me' on
the floor.
She drank the drink until she was tiny.
Finally, she opened the door to a world of wonder
and surprise.

Scarlett Shorter (10)

Great Milton CE Primary School, Oxford

Wonderland

W onderful things kept inside
O oh, how I'd love you by my side
N ever doubt the wonders it may hold
D on't choose wrong or you'll go bald
E verlasting pet of doom
R iver made of gummy gloom
L and of opportunity awaits
A wrong move will lead to your fate
N ever steal, just go
D id you know, this winter will snow?

Millie McCann (10)
Great Milton CE Primary School, Oxford

The Weather

The sun shines here,
The moon gleams there,
Somewhere there's rain
And heat we can't bear.

Somewhere it's snowing,
With beautiful flakes,
Somewhere there's a storm
That floods the rivers and lakes.

All the different weathers,
I hope they never go away,
The heat, the snow, the storms, the rain,
I hope they never go away!

Elda Parton (10)
Great Milton CE Primary School, Oxford

Swimming With Birds

I'm going to a dive
It's gonna be filmed live
I'm swimming with birds
I'm lost for words
At how this will work?

Oceans and rivers
Give me the quivers
I'm now stuck on this cliff edge
My feet are in a wedge.

I've got to do this dive
But how will I survive?
The birds are waiting for me down below,
Here I go!

Elliott Donald Flint Richardson (10)
Great Milton CE Primary School, Oxford

The Disco

I went to a disco today!
I had so much fun,
As we all danced away.

The lights danced along with us,
As they swept across the floor.
Our feet could not stop moving,
They just wanted more; more, more!

As the music hit our ears,
We all sang our best.
Everyone was so happy,
And now the night is over,
We all need a rest!

Tiger-Lee Coombes (10)
Great Milton CE Primary School, Oxford

If I Could...

If I could swim I would be happy,
Yes that's all I need.
But no, I can't do that
So I will just work with people that I need to feed.

If I could run I would be happy,
Yes, that's all I need.
But you see I can't do that either
Because I've just come down with a fever!

Eden Adiri (10)
Great Milton CE Primary School, Oxford

Imagine

I nside is where it comes from
M ade up by you
A ny little story to thought
G iven by the mind
I magine anything
N ever a limit
E verything is possible.

Harry Taylor (11)
Great Milton CE Primary School, Oxford

Dad In Bed

A blackout poem

Dad snored,
As quickly as he could,
Looking out of the window frame
There was no sound,
Not even the birds were singing yet.

Samuel Bridge (10)
Great Milton CE Primary School, Oxford

The Sugar Sweet Shop

I am right now in such a huff,
As no one will buy a single Lemon Puff,
I don't know why they are being so mean,
Is it because the shop isn't that clean?
I assure you now the floor is as clean as can be,
So maybe it's because of me.

Lemon Drops and Swirly Pops are as good as the
Fizzers,
And Freddos are the best - just like the Wizzers.
The flavours are amazing, now that is true,
Maybe my children could give me a clue.
I don't like this problem, not one little bit,
I am a dragon - maybe that's it!

Elisha Fernandez (10)
Grove CE Primary School, Grove

Wonderland

W onderlands are beautiful. All gummy bears and lollipops.

O nly a wonderland can have these things like gumballs and chocolate.

N obody can resist these amazing treats.

D ipping gummies in melted chocolate, yum!

E verybody eating candy and having fun.

R ainbow Smarties dropping from the sky.

L ittle Magic Stars all scrummy up high.

A ll candy is fantastic.

N obody can help but love its delicious taste.

D o you like candy?

Phoebe Miles (8)
Grove CE Primary School, Grove

Rainbow Ride

R unning on clouds, jumping through the sky. Suddenly I slipped on a rainbow slide.

A rainbow fell on my arm. Wake up you sleepy head!

I didn't want to wake up, kept sliding down the rainbow.

N o matter what I do, I still want to imagine fairies and rainbows.

B elieving is good to know.

O h my, oh my, oh no, the rainbow began to fall.

W hat, did it fall? No it didn't, it's all in one piece.

Lily Sutton (7)
Grove CE Primary School, Grove

The Debate Over Pollination

"Excuse me!" shouts a tiny voice
To a bee, "Pollinate me, you have no choice!"

Says the bee, "I don't want to pollinate you!
I prefer tulips and roses and snowdrops too!"

The poor daffodil begins to cry.
The bee turns around and says, "My, oh my!"

The flower looks up and says with a sigh,
"Okay, okay! Fly away home and tell them you let
my species die."

Thomas L Reeves (10)
Grove CE Primary School, Grove

The Secret Garden

In my garden, I could see a door,
I opened the door and there were petals all over the floor.
I saw glittery trees and flowers that could talk,
The flowers said to me, "On you walk."
I could smell the clean fresh air,
There was a nice breeze and it made my hair go everywhere.
There was a boy called Billy,
We made necklaces out of lilies,
It was the best day ever.

Megan Zamora Rowe (8)
Grove CE Primary School, Grove

Candy Land

C andy Land is sweet and tasty, you will love the taste.

A lolly and a pop go together, making a lollipop.

N ice bees and peas.

D airy Milk, yum yum!

Y ou and me get some.

L ands are like my favourite land.

A pop is a lollipop.

N aughty if you're not invited.

D iet Coke, bad for you!

Francesca Grace Huggins (7)
Grove CE Primary School, Grove

Unicorn Ride

U nicorns can take you anywhere.
N o one knows that they exist.
I love unicorns, they are beautiful.
C ome and see her, she is in Wonderland.
O h no, oh no, a unicorn has crashed into the snow.
R ainbows are lovely, just like unicorns.
N o the unicorn did not crash, it is just that they like being looked at.

Aliceson Livingston (7)
Grove CE Primary School, Grove

Volcano Surf

V olcanoes are very boiling hot.

O n the volcano there is orange stuff, is it ear wax?

L ove the lava, you can surf.

C an you eat and drink lava.

A nd can you swim in it?

N o, it will burn you.

O h no, I did it!

Maizie Liverbeth (7)
Grove CE Primary School, Grove

Genie

G enie made me a ginormous dragon.

E xcellent witches the genie gave me. Explore the genie.

N ever fight with a genie.

I n caves there's magic.

E nd of genies, it's sad.

S urprising sweets!

Ava Sherriff (7)
Grove CE Primary School, Grove

Easter

E ggs are yummy to eat.

A ll go hunting for eggs.

S ome people get an Easter basket.

T he Easter bunny gives the children toys or teddies.

E ggs over Easter.

R eady for Easter!

Summer Carter (7)
Grove CE Primary School, Grove

Aliens

A liens love humans
L ions hate space
I n the spaceship, they are planning
E vil aliens make a plan
N ever trust aliens
S even is the name of their commander.

Samuel (7)
Grove CE Primary School, Grove

Mammoths

M ammoths are mammals
A nd giant
M unching leaves
M assive long, big tusks
O ld
T ails are short
H airy, muddy, brown
S tompy feet.

Kayden Rowbottom (7)

Grove CE Primary School, Grove

Friends

F un games.
R espect them.
I trust them.
E verybody needs friends.
N ever disrespect.
D o you have many friends?
S o many friends.

Thomas Perkins (7)
Grove CE Primary School, Grove

Zebra

Z ebras are very wild
E verybody was eating grass
B aby zebras are being born
R ainbows shining over animals
A zebra is stripy.

Hannah Sear (7)
Grove CE Primary School, Grove

School

S chool is fun.
C heerful place.
H elpful people.
O h no, I'm locked in.
O ranges are nice.
L ove is nice.

Joshua Norris (7)
Grove CE Primary School, Grove

Pug

P is for party time
U is for Uggs, comfy shoes
G is for good people.

Rudi Jenkins (8)

Grove CE Primary School, Grove

Alien Cookie Dragon

A lien cookie dragon loves to play.
L ittle did he know a bear's on the way!
I n his car he rode away!
E nergy lost, he fell in hay!
"N o!" he screamed and ran again!

C ounting our time in dismay!
O n a plane far away.
"O h no," he said, "my cookies!"
K arate chop! He's gone and back!
I n his head it's time to snap!
E ven if it is a trap!

D on't I say on the plane,
"R emake them again and again,
A gain and again," he said with a frown.
"G o on try, it'll be fun."
"O kay," he said and try he did.
N ow we're eating cookies in Hawaii!

Samrah Shah (10)
Wood Farm Primary School, Headington

Flora's Butt's Exploding!

U nbelievable Jeff,
N o, no, no, my unicorn is farting
I n my face!
C ome on, I'm taking you to the vet.
O kay, we're at the vet.
R eady, steady, wait, hide. *Prrr!* Oh my god,
N ooo! I can't breathe.

F lora, you are the biggest stink bomb on Earth.
A mazingly I survive!
R ight, what are you doing now?
T rying to eat more chocolate cookies.
S top, stop, stop, no more cookies now!

F rightful farts from Flora.
L ike this.
O kay, stay away, if you don't you will stink.
R ight, she absolutely pongs.
A fter a million years she still stinks.

Alyssa Boyce Hall (9)
Wood Farm Primary School, Headington

BBQ On The Sun

B ig fat aliens getting fried
B undle of animals that have died
Q uestions asked, all are why?

O ther people just are shy.
N o one else even tries.

T he aliens are all now deep fried.
H ow are they all crispy and wide?
E lephants deep fried as well

S ize of 66 buses
U nder-sized aliens
N icholas the alien fried the best.

Dominik Ivancik (10)
Wood Farm Primary School, Headington

Unicorn Dancing Homework Book

Work with a dancing homework book
It's hard but fun while eating chewing gum
White and red make pink
I love ice cream in a sink
Don't shout or cry
I've been spelling, why?
My homework book is rude but nice
It does not like chicken, nice!
I say yes, it says no
I say, let it go!
My dancing unicorn homework book!

Sienna Rowe (9)

Wood Farm Primary School, Headington

A Shiny Unicorn Was Jumping

They like eating jam.
They don't like Spam.
They are also white and pink.
They can sink.
They make friends a lot.
They're like a robot.
Their wings are really pretty
And they live in the city.
Today is the day
And I feel okay.
I'm the unicorn who likes to play
And I play every day.

Mya Evans (10)
Wood Farm Primary School, Headington

Energetic Football Swimming

I saw my football swimming so fast
Everywhere around the pool
And I put on my flying swimming suit,
I tried to catch it
But it was so fast I always missed it.
So I made a machine of wonder
And I caught it
And it was so energetic,
That's so cool!

Mohamed (9)
Wood Farm Primary School, Headington

Burger Mania

In Burger Mania
Burgers run around wildly.
You can see burgers scurrying,
Playing football,
Cooking BBQs outside
And eating chocolate cookies,
Drinking burger Coke,
Flying green UFOs,
Also big burger cars
And there are black and red burgers!

Harry Stillman (9)
Wood Farm Primary School, Headington

A Fierce Pooping Unicorn

A fierce unicorn,
Was walking down the street,
He was eating and jumping,
He felt a little weird,
Because he felt like pooping,
He pooped and pooped,
He kept on doing it,
It became smelly,
It became angry,
It all became a disaster!

Mitul Gupta (9)
Wood Farm Primary School, Headington

My Silly Little Unicorn

There's a unicorn that is shiny,
With lots of beauty,
His horn has a sparkle,
Although he is a unicorn he swims with mermaids,
He eats burgers, his favourite food,
He lives with a stinky, weird dragon,
In his old and crusty castle.

Iman Zia (9)
Wood Farm Primary School, Headington

My Dangerous Dancing Teacher

My teacher is dancing
What do I do?
She is twirling and whirling,
Right next to you.
She eats a mango
Whilst doing the tango.
The students are horrified,
They need a break.
The bell now rang,
Let's quickly escape!

Adina Nadeem-Aftab (9)
Wood Farm Primary School, Headington

Eating Glittery Clouds

Scrumptious, shimmery candyfloss.
I like cookies and I'm the boss.
Be aware in the night because the clouds might bite!
The clouds are hunting day and night,
I am telling you, beware because the clouds might take a bite!

Haniya Khanum Siddique (10)
Wood Farm Primary School, Headington

My Naughty Minion

M y naughty Minion, eating KFC.

I nside a tidal wave.

N othing can compare to the Minions over there.

I ce cream for after.

O n the beach.

N aughty Minions, as happy as can be.

Camron Betnay (10)
Wood Farm Primary School, Headington

Mars Bars On Planet Mars

Mars bars grow on Mars
and they will never stop.
But you have to be aware
because they won't let you there.
Stars also grow there like my little bars.
So if you dare to shout at them
they will bite you!

Huda Boucetta (10)

Wood Farm Primary School, Headington

Unicorns

Unicorns are shiny, glittery too
Unicorns, beautiful, flying
Spitting candy out their mouths
Unicorns, unicorns, joy
Having the best time
Spin, spin, spin
Unicorns, unicorns,
This poem is done!

Tawhida Al-Jannath (9)
Wood Farm Primary School, Headington

Football With Messi

Teams are fighting for the win...
Going for midfield.
Getting marked.
Finding the position.
Tackle for the ball.
It's a foul.
It's a penalty
And he scores!

Mohammed Siddiq (10)
Wood Farm Primary School, Headington

Chocolate Wonderland

The chocolate land is full of sweets
But I didn't know what to eat.
So I flew in the sky with all the candyfloss clouds
So I could see the beautiful view.

Shania Darcy Lewis (10)
Wood Farm Primary School, Headington

Mountain Cake

My favourite cake is the mountain cake.
It is very yummy, yummy and nice!
It's really delicious and colourful
And sparkly and spangly as well!

Rasjhad Kanbus (10)
Wood Farm Primary School, Headington

Young Writers Information

We hope you have enjoyed reading this book – and that you will continue to in the coming years.

If you're a young writer who enjoys reading and creative writing, or the parent of an enthusiastic poet or story writer, do visit our website **www.youngwriters.co.uk**. Here you will find free competitions, workshops and games, as well as recommended reads, a poetry glossary and our blog. There's lots to keep budding writers motivated to write!

If you would like to order further copies of this book, or any of our other titles, then please give us a call or visit **www.youngwriters.co.uk**.

Young Writers
Remus House
Coltsfoot Drive
Peterborough
PE2 9BF
(01733) 890066
info@youngwriters.co.uk

Join in the conversation!
Tips, news, giveaways and much more!

 YoungWritersUK    @YoungWritersCW